How to Make Smoothies:

Simple, Easy and Healthy Blender Recipes

Cathy L. Kidd

The cover photo pictures (from left to right): Orange Banana
Cream, Arugula Ginger, Berry, Eggnog and Sparkling Fruit in
the center.

First Printing, 2012
Printed in the United States of America

Table of Contents

Introduction

Smoothies have been very popular for years for good reason. They are simple and easy to make, nutritious and flexible to adjustment for your favorite tastes. You can drink them as complete meal replacements or as an alternative to soda or another sugary beverage with your meal. The smoothies that contain banana are especially filling.

If you like you can consider the recipes in this book as starting places for your own creations and let your creative "juices" flow!

As you try the recipes, you may need to adjust the quantity of the ingredients to suit the size of your blender. The servings for each recipe are for one unless otherwise stated although you may find some of the single servings are pretty large. With a little experimenting and experience you will get the quantities just right! If you make more than one serving at a time, you can always freeze the left over portion for later. When you're ready to drink it, refrigerate it until defrosted and then blend again before drinking.

Some tips to make your smoothie its best and most tasty:
- Use fresh juice, not concentrate when you can.
- If you like it really cold, use frozen fruit.
- Drink it freshly made for it to be at its best.
- The yogurt smoothies can be very thick and hard to blend for some blenders. You can add a little low fat milk to make it easier to mix and a little less thick.
- Be aware that if you use a lot of raspberries and blackberries in your smoothie, you'll also get a lot of the seeds too. It will not be a smooth smoothie! But if you like a little crunch, use them freely.
- If you choose to use frozen fruit and there is not a lot of liquid in the recipe, you can defrost the fruit for a few minutes in warm water so it will blend better.

So there you have it – couldn't be more simple or easy. Whip up a smoothie today and enjoy!

The Recipes

Apple

2 cup	Applesauce
1 cup	Apple cider
1 cup	Orange juice
2 tablespoon	Maple syrup
1/2 teaspoon	Nutmeg
1/2 teaspoon	Cinnamon

Combine all of the ingredients in a blender and blend until smooth. Makes 2 servings.

Apple Cinnamon

3/4 cup	Apple sugarfree syrup
1/4 cup	Cinnamon sugarfree syrup
2 scoops	Vege Fuel
1 1/2 cups	Crushed ice
1/4 cup	Heavy cream (optional)

Combine all of the ingredients in a blender and blend until smooth.

Note: Vege Fuel is a soy protein dietary supplement often used by vegetarians and athletes. It is a superior source of quality protein that is low fat, cholesterol and lactose free and contains no aspartame. It can promote muscle growth and nitrogen retention.

Apple Coconut

1/4 cup	Apple juice
1 pinch	Coconut, grated or
	1 tablespoon coconut milk
1/2	Banana
1/4 teaspoon	Fresh ginger root, peeled
2 small	Ice cubes

Combine all of the ingredients in a blender and blend until smooth.

Apple Maple

2 cups	Applesauce
1 cup	Apple cider
1 cup	Orange juice
2 tablespoons	Vermont maple syrup
1/2 teaspoon	Nutmeg
1/2 teaspoon	Cinnamon

Combine all of the ingredients in a blender and blend until smooth.

Apple Raspberry Strawberry

1 cup	Apple juice
1 1/2 cups	Lemonade
1 cup	Frozen raspberries
1/2 cup	Frozen strawberries
1 cup	Raspberry sherbet

Combine all of the ingredients in a blender and blend until smooth. Serves 3-5.

Banana Apricot

1 cup	Ripe bananas, mashed, frozen
1 cup	Apricot nectar
1/2 cup	Low fat milk
1/4 teaspoon	Vanilla

Combine all of the ingredients in a blender and blend until smooth. Serves 2.

Banana Lime

1	Banana
2 cups	Limeade
1 cup	Lime sherbet
3 Tablespoons	Coconut milk
1 cup	Ice

Combine all of the ingredients in a blender and blend until smooth. Serves 3-5.

Banana Mango

1/2 cup	Banana; sliced
1/2 cup	Mango, cut into pieces
2 cups	Milk
1 tablespoon	Honey

Combine all of the ingredients in a blender and blend until smooth. Serves 3.

Note: For variety you can substitute papaya or guava for the mango.

Banana Oat

1	Banana, cut in pieces
1 packet	Instant oatmeal, regular flavor
1 cup	Milk
1 cup	Orange Juice

Combine all of the ingredients in a blender and blend until smooth.

Banana Orange Tangerine

2 medium	Bananas, quartered
1 pint	orange sorbet or
	2 cups orange sherbet, slightly softened
1 cup	Mandarin Tangerine juice

Combine all of the ingredients in a blender and blend until smooth. Garnish with orange slices and curls if desired.

Banana Peach

1 cup	Ripe bananas, mashed, frozen
1 cup	Peach nectar
1/2 cup	Low fat milk

Combine all of the ingredients in a blender and blend until smooth. Serves 2.

Banana Peach Strawberry

2	Bananas, frozen
1 cup	Frozen peaches, sliced
1/2 cup	Strawberries, sliced
1 cup	Apple juice

Combine all of the ingredients in a blender and blend until smooth.

Note: For variety you can add 1/8 teaspoon of cinnamon.

Banana Peanut Butter

1/3 small	Banana
1 tablespoon	Reduced fat peanut butter
8 ounces	Skim milk
2 packages	Sugar substitute
5	Ice cubes

Combine all of the ingredients except for the ice cubes in a blender and blend until smooth. Add the ice cubes and blend again.

Banana Pineapple

1/2	Banana
1/2 cup	Pineapple chunks
1/2 cup	Pineapple juice
1/2 cup	Ice cubes
1 tablespoon	Sugar
1/4 teaspoon	Coconut extract

Combine all of the ingredients in a blender and blend until smooth.

Banana Strawberry

2	Bananas, frozen
1 cup	Strawberries
1 cup	Vanilla rice milk
1 teaspoon	Vanilla Extract
4 tablespoons	Maple Syrup
1/10 teaspoon	Nutmeg

Combine all of the ingredients in a blender and blend until smooth.

Banana Strawberry Orange

1	Banana, sliced
1/2 cup	Strawberries
1/2 cup	Orange juice
3-5	Ice cubes

Combine all of the ingredients in a blender and blend until smooth.

Blueberry Banana

1/4-1/2 cup	Frozen blueberries
1/2	Banana, frozen
1/2-3/4 cup	Rice milk
1/2 teaspoon	Vanilla extract
1 package	Sweetner

Combine all of the ingredients in a blender and blend until smooth.

Blueberry Buttermilk

1/2 cup	Frozen blueberries
1 cup	Buttermilk
1	Ripe banana, cut into pieces
1 tablespoon	Granulated sugar
4	Ice cubes

Combine all of the ingredients in a blender and blend until smooth. Serves 2

Boysenberry Blueberry

1 1/2 cups	Boysenberry flavored juice
1 cup	Boysenberries
1 cup	Blueberries, frozen

Combine all of the ingredients in a blender and blend until smooth. Serves 2

Note: If you can't find boysenberries, you can substitute blackberries.

Breakfast Fruit

1/2 cup	Orange juice
1	Banana
6-7	Frozen strawberries
4-5 slices	Frozen peaches
5-6 frozen	Blueberries
6-7	Ice cubes
1 teaspoon	Honey (optional)
Dash	Nutmeg (optional)
	Fresh mint (optional)

Combine all of the ingredients except the ice cubes, mint and nutmeg in a blender and blend until smooth. Add the ice, and blend again. Pour into a glass and sprinkle the nutmeg on top. Garnish with the fresh mint.

Cantaloupe Cherry

1/2	Cantaloupe, peeled, seeded, and sliced
2-3	Cherries, pitted
1/2 cup	Apple or apricot juice
1/4 cup	Raspberries or blackberries
3-4	Ice cubes

Combine all of the ingredients in a blender and blend until smooth.

Cherry Vanilla

1/4 cup	Cherry sugarfree syrup
1/4 cup	Vanilla Sugarfree syrup
2 scoops	Vege Fuel
1 1/2 cups	Crushed ice

Combine all of the ingredients in a blender and blend until smooth.

Note: Vege Fuel is a soy protein dietary supplement often used by vegetarians and athletes. It is a superior source of quality protein that is low fat, cholesterol and lactose free and contains no aspartame. It can promote muscle growth and nitrogen retention.

Chocolate

1/2 bar	Milk chocolate
2 scoops	Chocolate ice cream
1/2 cup	Milk
3-5	Ice cubes

Combine all of the ingredients except the ice cubes in a blender and blend until smooth. Add the ice cubes and blend again. Serves 2.

Cranberry Raspberry Orange

1 cup	Cranberry juice
1/2 cup	Raspberry sorbet
1 tablespoon	Orange juice concentrate
1 1/2 cup	Orange sections
1/2 cup	Fresh cranberries

Combine the cranberry juice, sorbet, and orange juice concentrate in a blender and blend until smooth. Add the orange sections and cranberries and blend again. Serves 2.

Fresh Fruit

1/2 cup	Watermelon, cut in pieces
1/2 cup	Cantaloupe or Honeydew melon, cut in pieces
1/2 cup	Pineapple, cut in pieces
1/2 cup	Mango, cut in pieces
1 cup	Strawberries, halved
1/8 cup	Sugar
1/2 cup	Orange Juice
	Crushed Ice

Mix all of the ingredients except the ice. Fill the blender container 1/2 full of the mixture. Add crushed ice to fill to the top. Cover and blend on high speed until blended. Repeat with the remaining mixture. Serves 3.

Fruit Salad

1 medium	Ripe peach
3/4 cup	Strawberries, fresh or frozen
1/2	Banana
2 cup	Skimmed evaporated milk, chilled
4 teaspoon	Frozen orange juice concentrate
1 t	Vanilla
4-6	ice cubes
	Cinnamon (optional)

Combine all of the ingredients except the ice cubes and cinnamon in a blender and blend until smooth. Add the ice cubes one at a time while blending. Pour into glasses and sprinkle with cinnamon. Serves 4.

Fruit Cocktail

1 (8 oz.) can	Fruit cocktail, chilled, not drained
1 cup	Milk
1/4 cup	Nonfat dry milk powder
1/2 teaspoon	Vanilla
1/2 cup	Ice cubes
	Cinnamon, ground (optional)

Combine all of the ingredients except the ice cubes in a blender and blend until smooth. Add the ice cubes and blend again. Pour into glasses and sprinkle with cinnamon. Serves 4.

Gala Apple

1	Gala apple, peeled, cored and chopped
1	Banana, frozen and chopped
1/2 cup	Orange juice
1/4 cup	Nonfat milk

Combine all of the ingredients in a blender and blend until smooth. Serves 2.

Ginger

1/4-1/2 teaspoon	Fresh ginger root, grated
1/2 cup	Orange juice
1/4 cup	Pineapple juice
1/2	Banana
1/2 cup	Crushed ice

Combine all of the ingredients in a blender and blend until smooth.

Grape

2 cups	Red seedless grapes
1 cup	Green seedless grapes
1/2 cup	Purple grape juice
2 teaspoons	Lime juice
1 teaspoon	Fresh ginger root, peeled and minced
3	Ice cubes

Combine all of the ingredients in a blender and blend until smooth.

Island Fruit

1 small	Banana, cut into pieces
2 tablespoons	Coconut milk
2 tablespoons	Lime juice
1/4 cup	Orange juice
1/4 cup	Pineapple juice
1/2 teaspoon	Fresh ginger root, grated
3	Ice cubes

Combine all of the ingredients in a blender and blend until smooth.

Kiwi Lime (Version 1)

1 1/2 cups	Kiwi, peeled, diced
1 1/2 cups	Lime sherbet
1 cup	Ripe banana, diced
1 cup	Honeydew melon

Combine all of the ingredients in a blender and blend until smooth.

Kiwi Lime (Version 2)

2	Kiwi, peeled, cut into pieces
1	Banana, cut into pieces
1 teaspoon	Lime juice
1/2 teaspoon	Lime zest, grated
2	Ice cubes
1 cup	Skim milk
1/4 cup	Part skim milk ricotta cheese

Combine the fruit, juice, zest and ice cubes in a blender and blend until smooth. Add the milk and ricotta and blend for another 5-10 seconds, scraping down the sides of the container with a rubber spatula. Serves 2.

Kiwi Strawberry

3	Kiwi, peeled
1/2 cup	Frozen strawberries
1 cup	Frozen banana, sliced
3/4 cup	Pineapple juice

Combine all of the ingredients in a blender and blend until smooth.

Lemon Cucumber

1 cup	Lemon sorbet
1	Cucumber, peeled, seeded and chopped
1 1/2 cups	Apple juice or cider
3 tablespoons	Mint leaves, finely chopped
1 cup	Ice cubes

Combine all of the ingredients in a blender and blend until smooth. Serves 2.

Mango Orange

1/2 cup	Mango, peeled, pitted and sliced
1/2 cup	Orange juice
	Honey to taste
1/2 cup	Ice

Combine all of the ingredients except the ice in a blender and blend until smooth. Add the ice and blend again.

Mango Peach

1 cup	Mango, peeled and cut into pieces
1 large	Peach, peeled, pitted, and cut into pieces
1 cup	Peach nectar
2 tablespoons	Lime juice

Combine all of the ingredients in a blender and blend until smooth. Serves 2.

Mango Pineapple Banana

1 1/2 cups	Frozen mango slices
1 cup	Pineapple juice
1 cup	Orange juice
1/2	Banana, cut into pieces, frozen
1 cup	Pineapple sherbet

Combine all of the ingredients in a blender and blend until smooth. Serves 3-5.

Mango Strawberry

2	Mangos, peeled and cut into pieces
1 cup	Strawberries, sliced
1 cup	Orange juice
2 tablespoons	Maple syrup
1/3 teaspoon	Cinnamon
1/4 tablespoon	Vanilla extract
1 cup	Crushed ice

Combine all of the ingredients in a blender and blend until smooth.

Mango Strawberry Carrot Banana

1	Mango, peeled and cut into pieces
8 large	Strawberries
2 medium	Carrots, chopped
2	Bananas, cut into pieces
2 cups	Ice cubes
1 tablespoon	Honey
1 cup	Yogurt (optional)

Combine all of the ingredients in a blender and blend until smooth. Serves 2.

Note: If you use the yogurt, you may need to do this one in two batches depending on the size of your blender.

Melon Mint

2 cups	Cantaloupe, diced
1 cup	Honeydew melon, diced
1 cup	Watermelon, seeded, diced
1/2 cup	Passion fruit or mango juice
1 tablespoon	Lime juice
2 teaspoons	Honey
10	Fresh mint leaves
3	Ice cubes

Combine all of the ingredients in a blender and blend until smooth. Serves 2.

Nectarine Berry

1	Nectarine, pitted, cut into pieces
3/4 cup	Strawberries, hulled
3/4 cup	Blueberries, rinsed and drained
1/3 cup	Nonfat dry milk powder
1 cup	Crushed ice

Combine all of the ingredients in a blender and blend until smooth.

Orange

3 ounces	Orange juice concentrate, frozen
1/2 cup	Milk
1/2 cup	Water
1/8 cup	Sugar
1/4 teaspoon	Vanilla
5	Ice cubes, crushed

Combine all of the ingredients in a blender and blend until smooth. Serves 3.

Orange Banana Cream

1/4 cup	Orange juice
1/2	Banana
1/4 cup	Pineapple juice
1 tbsp	Coconut milk
1/4 teaspoon	Fresh ginger root, grated
1/2 cup	Crushed ice or 2 small ice cubes

Combine all of the ingredients in a blender and blend until smooth.

Note: This is the smoothie pictured at the start of this section.

Orange Banana Peach Raspberry

1 1/2 cups	Orange juice, freshly squeezed
1 medium	Banana, cut into pieces
1	Ripe peach, peeled, pitted, and diced
1 cup	Raspberries
3	Ice cubes

Combine all of the ingredients in a blender and blend until smooth. Serves 2.

Orange Pineapple Coconut

1/4 cup	Orange juice
1/4 cup	Pineapple juice
1 tablespoon	Coconut milk
1/2	Banana
1/4 teaspoon	Fresh ginger root, peeled, grated
1/2 cup	Crushed ice or 2 small ice cubes

Combine all of the ingredients in a blender and blend until smooth.

Orange Pineapple Ginger

1/2 cup	Orange juice
1/4 cup	Pineapple juice
1/2	Banana
1/4 teaspoon	Fresh ginger root, peeled, grated
1/2 cup	Ice, crushed

Combine all of the ingredients in a blender and blend until smooth.

Orange Strawberry Pineapple

1 cup	Orange sherbet
1 cup	Fresh strawberries
1 1/3 cups	Pineapple chunks, fresh or canned in juice and drained
1 1/2 cups	Mineral water

Combine all of the ingredients except the mineral water in a blender and blend until smooth. Add mineral water and blend again. Serves 4.

Papaya

3/4 cup	Papaya, peeled, seeded and chopped
1/2 cup	Orange juice
1/2 cup	Ice
	Honey to taste

Combine all of the ingredients except the ice in a blender and blend until smooth. Add the ice and blend again.

Papaya Raspberry

1/2	Papaya, peeled, seeded and chopped
10-12	Raspberries (fresh or frozen)
1	Banana, frozen
1/2 cup	Water or fruit juice
1 tablespoon	Wheat germ, toasted (optional)

Combine all of the ingredients in a blender and blend until smooth.

Peach

1	Frozen peach slices
1/3 cup	Nonfat milk
1/4 cup	Frozen apple juice concentrate

Combine all of the ingredients in a blender and blend until smooth.

Peach Orange Almond

1 cup	Orange juice
1 cup	Frozen peaches
1	Banana, cut into pieces, frozen
2 tablespoons	Slivered almonds, toasted

Combine all of the ingredients in a blender and blend until smooth.

Note: For variety you can use pecans instead of the almonds and pineapple juice instead of the orange juice.

Peach Strawberry

3-5 slices	Peach
4 large	Strawberries
1	Banana
10 ounces	Apple cider
1/8 teaspoon	Cinnamon

Combine all of the ingredients in a blender and blend until smooth.

Pina Colada

5 tablespoons	Coconut milk
2 1/2 cups	Pineapple juice
1/2 cup	Vanilla ice cream
1/2	Banana, cut into pieces, frozen
1 1/2 cups	Frozen pineapple chunks

Combine all of the ingredients in a blender and blend until smooth. Serves 3-5.

Pineapple

1 (20 oz.) can	Unsweetened pineapple chunks
1 cup	Buttermilk
2 teaspoon	Vanilla extract
2 teaspoon	Liquid sweetener
	Mint leaves (optional)

Drain the pineapple, reserving 1/2 cup of the juice. Freeze the pineapple chunks. Combine all of the ingredients including the reserved juice in a blender and blend until smooth. Serve garnished with the mint if desired.

Pineapple Banana

6 slices	Canned pineapple
2	Bananas, frozen and cut into pieces
2 cups	Nonfat milk
1 tablespoon	Honey

Combine all of the ingredients in a blender and blend until smooth. Serves 2.

Pineapple Cantaloupe

1 1/2 cups	Pineapple, diced
1 1/2 cups	Cantaloupe, diced
1/2 cup	Orange juice, freshly squeezed
1/2 cup	Carrot juice
Pinch	Nutmeg
3	Ice cubes

Combine all of the ingredients in a blender and blend until smooth. Serves 2.

Pineapple Coconut

1/2 cup	Buttermilk
1 cup	Canned pineapple chunks, drained
1 teaspoon	Coconut flakes
1/2 teaspoon	Coconut extract

Combine all of the ingredients in a blender and blend until smooth.

Pineapple Papaya

1/4 cup	Fresh pineapple, peeled, cored and cut into pieces
1/4 cup	Ripe papaya, peeled, seeded and chopped
1/2 cup	Orange juice
	Honey to taste
1/2 cup	Ice

Combine all of the ingredients except the ice in a blender and blend until smooth. Add the ice and blend again.

Pineapple Strawberry

3/4 cup	Pineapple juice, chilled
1 cup	Fresh strawberries
1	Ripe banana
	Ice cubes

Combine all of the ingredients in a blender and blend until smooth.

Pumpkin

1 3/4 cups	Canned pumpkin, chilled
12 ounces	Evaporated skim milk, chilled
1 1/2 cups	Orange juice
1/2 cup	Banana, cut into pieces
1/3 cup	Brown sugar

Combine all of the ingredients in a blender and blend until smooth. Serves 6.

Raspberry Peach

10 ounces	Frozen raspberries in light syrup, thawed
1 cup	Peach Nectar
1/2 cup	Buttermilk
1 tablespoon	Honey

Combine all of the ingredients in a blender and blend until smooth. Serves 4.

Red, White and Blueberry

1/4 cup	Blueberries
1/4 cup	Blackberries
1	Banana
1/2 cup	Apple juice
1/3 cup	Raspberry sorbet

Combine all of the ingredients in a blender and blend until smooth.

Strawberry Apple Blueberry Peach

1/2 cup	Strawberries, sliced
2	Apples peeled, cored and cut into pieces
1/2 cup	Blueberries
1/2 cup	Peaches
3/4cup	Apple juice
3/4cup	Orange juice

Combine all of the ingredients in a blender and blend until smooth.

Strawberry Banana

1 cup	Frozen strawberries
1 cup	Banana, frozen, cut into pieces
1 cup	Pineapple juice
2 tablespoons	Cream of coconut
1 dash	Grenadine

Combine all of the ingredients in a blender and blend until smooth. Add more pineapple juice if needed to reach desired consistency. Serves 2.

Strawberry Peach Pear

1 cup	Frozen strawberries, slightly thawed
1	Fresh peach, sliced
1	Pear, peeled, cored, chopped
1 tablespoon	Lime juice

Combine all of the ingredients in a blender and blend until smooth. Serves 2.

Strawberry Raspberry Banana

1 1/2 cups	Ripe strawberries, sliced
1 cup	Raspberries
1	Banana, sliced
1 cup	Orange juice, freshly squeezed

Combine all of the ingredients in a blender and blend until smooth. Serves 2

Strawberry Lemon

5 ounces	Frozen strawberries, thawed
2 cups	Milk
1/2 pint	Strawberry ice cream
1/2 teaspoon	Lemon rind, grated

Combine all of the ingredients in a blender and blend until smooth. Serves 4.

Note: Depending on the size of your blender, you may need to do this one in two parts.

Tropical Fruit

1 large	Banana, cut into pieces
2	Kiwi, peeled, diced
1/2 cup	Mango, peeled, diced
1/2 cup	Papaya, peeled, diced
1 cup	Orange juice, freshly squeezed
3	Ice cubes

Combine all of the ingredients in a blender and blend until smooth. Serves 2

Papaya Peach Passion Fruit

1	Papaya, peeled, seeded, sliced
1	Peach, sliced
2	Passion fruit, pulp and seeds
5 ounces	Orange juice, freshly squeezed

Combine all of the ingredients in a blender and blend until smooth. Serves 2

Note: The Passion fruit seeds add extra antioxidant value to this smoothie so be sure to include them.

Wild Berry

1 cup	Orange juice
1/4 cup	Pineapple juice
2	Pineapple slices
6	Fresh strawberries
15	Frozen raspberries
10	Frozen blackberries
15	Frozen blueberries
	Ice cubes

Combine all of the ingredients in a blender and blend until smooth.

Soy Smoothies

These recipes include soy milk, and in some cases, tofu. Adding soy gives you a number of extra health benefits. It is a good protein source, is low fat and includes other nutrients like iron, calcium, and riboflavin. It's also an excellent alternative if you are lactose intolerant or a vegan.

Soy not only has health benefits, but it's good for our environment too. Growing soybeans uses fewer resources than raising cows and is a sustainable resource.

So if you've never tried soy milk before, these recipes are a great place to start!

Apple Banana

2	Ripe bananas, peeled, halved
2	Apples, peeled, cored, quartered
1 (10 oz.) container	Nonfat yogurt
2 tablespoons	Sugar
15 ounces	Soy milk

Combine all of the ingredients in a blender and blend until smooth.

Banana Molasses

5	Prunes, pitted
1 medium	Banana, peeled, cut into 1 inch pieces
2 cups	Low fat vanilla soy milk
1 tablespoon	Molasses
1/4 teaspoon	Ground cardamom
3	Ice cubes

Place the prunes in a small bowl and cover with hot tap water. Let them soak for 15 minutes or until plump. Drain.

Combine the prunes with the remaining ingredients in blender and blend until smooth.

Banana Soy

3/4 cup	Soy milk
1/2 cup	Soft silken tofu
4	Bananas, frozen
1 tablespoon	Honey
1 tablespoon	Vanilla extract
1 tablespoon	Carob powder

Combine soy milk and tofu in blender. Add the rest of the ingredients and blend until smooth.

Berry

1 cup	Blackberries
1 cup	Strawberries, halved
1 cup	Blueberries
1 cup	Low fat vanilla soymilk
1/8 teaspoon	Ground cinnamon
3	Ice cubes

Combine all of the ingredients in a blender and blend until smooth. Serves 2.

Note: This is the smoothie pictured at the start of this section.

Cantaloupe Strawberry Peanut Butter

1 cup	Nonfat soy milk
1/2 cup	Cantaloupe
1/2 cup	Strawberries, fresh or frozen (without sugar)
1 tablespoon	Peanut butter
1	Banana

Combine all of the ingredients in a blender and blend until smooth.

Chocolate Peanut Butter Banana

1	Banana
2 tablespoons	Peanut butter
1-2 squirts	Hershey's low calorie chocolate syrup
1 tablespoon	Wheat germ
6 ounces	Soy milk

Combine all of the ingredients in a blender and blend until smooth.

Fruit Spice

1	Banana, frozen, cut into 1-inch pieces
1/2-1 cup	Strawberries
1/4-1/2 cup	Soy milk
	Cinnamon to taste

Combine all of the ingredients in a blender and blend until smooth.

Note: Adjust the amount of strawberries and soy milk for a thicker or thinner smoothie. For variety, you can substitute orange juice or water for the soy milk, and peaches, blueberries, apple slices or more bananas for the strawberries. In addition to the cinnamon you can add nutmeg, cloves, ginger, or vanilla. Experiment with different combinations according to your taste.

Hawaiian

1 cup	Soy milk
1/2 cup	Pineapple juice
1	Banana, frozen
1 tablespoon	Maple syrup
2 tablespoons	Nonfat dry milk
1 tablespoon	Coconut milk
	Ice cubes

Combine all of the ingredients except the ice in a blender and blend until smooth. Add the ice and blend again.

Peanut Butter

1/2 cup	Soy milk
1/2 cup	Silken tofu
1/3 cup	Peanut butter
2	Bananas, frozen
2 tablespoons	Chocolate syrup

Combine all of the ingredients in a blender and blend until smooth. Serves 2.

Pumpkin Pie Spice

1 cup	Soy or almond milk
1/2 cup	Canned pumpkin
1/2	Banana
1/2 teaspoon	Maple syrup or honey
1/2 teaspoon	Vanilla extract
1/2 teaspoon	Ground pumpkin pie spice
	Whipped topping (optional)

Combine all of the ingredients in a blender and blend until smooth.

Note: Garnish with whipped topping if desired for the pumpkin pie effect.

Strawberry

1 cup	Vanilla soy milk
5 ounces	Silken tofu, firm, chilled and cubed
2 cups	Strawberries, frozen or fresh
2 tablespoons	Honey
1/2 teaspoon	Vanilla

Combine all of the ingredients in a blender and blend until smooth. Serves 2.

Yogurt Smoothies

All of these recipes include yogurt in some form. Some of them even use frozen yogurt, yum!!

The addition of yogurt makes your smoothie more creamy and tangy. It also adds the healthy benefits associated with yogurt including protein, vitamin D, calcium and probiotics.

If you are a vegetarian or concerned about adding more protein to your diet, you can consider using Greek yogurt which has a higher protein content. Enjoy!

Apple Apricot Banana

1	Golden delicious apple, chopped
1 cup	Apple juice
4	Fresh apricots, pitted (skin optional)
1	Banana, peeled
3/4 cup	Plain or vanilla nonfat yogurt
10-12	Ice cubes
1 tablespoon	Honey

Combine all of the ingredients in a blender and blend until smooth.

Apricot Almond

1/2 cup	Almond milk, chilled
1/2 cup	Apricot preserves, chilled
1/8 teaspoon	Almond extract
1 (6 oz.) container	Vanilla yogurt

Combine all of the ingredients in a blender and blend until smooth.

Apricot Mango

1 (6 oz.) container	Nonfat apricot mango yogurt
1 cup	Sugar free lemonade
1/2	Banana
5-6	Canned apricot halves

Combine all of the ingredients in a blender and blend until smooth.

Apricot Nectarine

1/2	Nectarine
1	Apricot
1 (6 oz.) container	Nonfat peach yogurt
4 ounces	Sugar free lemonade

Combine all of the ingredients in a blender and blend until smooth.

Apple Pie A-La-Mode

2 cups	Frozen nonfat vanilla yogurt
3/4 cup	Unsweetened applesauce
1/4 cup	Apple juice, chilled
1 cup	Apple, peeled, cored and diced
1/2 teaspoon	Cinnamon
1/4 teaspoon	Ground nutmeg

Combine all of the ingredients in a blender and blend until smooth.

Apple Strawberry

1/2 cup	Orange juice
1 cup	Fresh apple cider
4-6	Strawberries
1	Frozen Banana
1 cup	Nonfat yogurt (any fruit flavor)
1/4 cup	Almonds
2 tablespoons	Wheat germ

Combine all of the ingredients in a blender and blend until smooth. Serves 3.

Apricot

1/4 cup	Orange juice
1/2 cup	Plain low fat yogurt
1/2 cup	Fresh apricots, peeled, pitted and chopped
	Honey to taste

Combine all of the ingredients in a blender and blend until smooth.

Banana (Version 1)

1	Banana
1 cup	Plain yogurt
1 cup	Orange juice

Combine all of the ingredients in a blender and blend until smooth.

Note: You can add honey to taste if desired.

Banana (Version 2)

1	Banana
1/2 cup	Vanilla yogurt
2 cups	Milk
2 teaspoons	Vanilla extract

Combine all of the ingredients in a blender and blend until smooth.

Banana Blueberry

2	Bananas, sliced and frozen
1/2 cup	Blueberries
1 cup	Plain yogurt

Combine all of the ingredients in a blender and blend until smooth.

Banana Cinnamon

1/4 cup	Plain or vanilla yogurt
1/4 cup	Skim milk
1/2	Banana
1/8 teaspoon	Vanilla extract
1/8 teaspoon	Cinnamon
4	Ice cubes

Combine all of the ingredients in a blender and blend until smooth.

Note: For variety substitute whatever fruit is in season for the banana. You can also substitute nutmeg for the cinnamon.

Banana Coffee

2 small	Bananas, cut into pieces and frozen
1 1/2 cups	Skim milk
1 (8 oz.) container	Nonfat coffee yogurt
1/4 teaspoon	Ground cinnamon
1/8 teaspoon	Ground nutmeg

Combine all of the ingredients in a blender and blend until smooth.

Banana Orange

1	Banana, peeled, cut into pieces
1	Orange, peeled, cut into segments
1 (8 oz.) container	Nonfat cherry yogurt
8	Frozen dark cherries
6	Frozen strawberries

Combine all of the ingredients in a blender and blend until smooth. Serves 2.

Banana Peach Strawberry

1	Banana
3/4 cup	Frozen peaches
1 cup	Frozen strawberries
1 1/2 cup	Nonfat vanilla yogurt
1 tablespoon	Orange juice concentrate
10-12	Ice cubes

Combine all of the ingredients in a blender and blend until smooth. Serves 2.

Banana Strawberry

1/4 cup	Orange juice
1/2 cup	Plain nonfat yogurt
1/2 small	Ripe banana
1/4 cup	Strawberries, sliced
	Honey to taste
1 1/2 tablespoons	Vanilla soy protein powder

Combine all of the ingredients in a blender and blend until smooth.

Banana Strawberry Orange

1	Banana
4-6	Strawberries
1/2 cup	Orange juice
1 cup	Vanilla yogurt
1/2 cup	Milk
	Ice cubes

Combine all of the ingredients in a blender and blend until smooth. Serves 3.

Berry

1 (6 oz.) container	Nonfat yogurt (any flavor)
1 cup	Skim milk
1 cup	Frozen berries (any type or combination)

Combine all of the ingredients in a blender and blend until smooth.

Berry Banana

1/4 cup	Fresh or frozen assorted berries
1 small	Banana, cut into pieces and frozen
1 cup	Orange juice
3 tablespoons	Low fat vanilla yogurt
	Sliced fresh strawberries (optional)

Combine all of the ingredients in a blender and blend until smooth.

Note: You can use a combination of strawberries, blackberries, blueberries and/or raspberries as desired.

Black Cherry

1/2 cup	Frozen black cherries
5 tablespoons	Low fat vanilla or plain yogurt
	Honey to taste (optional)

Combine all of the ingredients in a blender and blend until smooth.

Blueberry

1 (6 oz.) container	Nonfat blueberry yogurt
1 cup	Blueberries
1 cup	Nonfat milk

Combine all of the ingredients in a blender and blend until smooth.

Blueberry Banana

3/4 cup	Fresh or frozen blueberries
1 medium	Ripe banana
1/4 cup	Nonfat vanilla yogurt
3/4 cup	Skim milk
Pinch	Cinnamon (if desired)
1/2 cup	Crushed ice

Combine all of the ingredients in a blender and blend until smooth.

Blueberry, Blackberry, Raspberry

1/6 cup	Blueberries
1/6 cup	Blackberries
1/6 cup	Raspberries
1/4 cup	Orange juice
1/2 cup	Plain low fat yogurt
	Honey to taste (optional)

Combine all of the ingredients in a blender and blend until smooth.

Blueberry Pineapple

2 cups	Fresh or frozen blueberries, chilled
1 cup	Pineapple/orange juice, or pineapple/strawberry juice, chilled
1 (8 oz.) container	Nonfat vanilla yogurt
1 tablespoon	Sugar or honey

Combine all of the ingredients in a blender and blend until smooth. Serves 3.

Cantaloupe

1/2	Ripe cantaloupe seeded and cut into pieces
1 cup	Skim milk
1 cup	Plain or vanilla fat free yogurt
1 cup	Ice, crushed
2 tablespoons	Sugar (or to taste)

Combine all of the ingredients in a blender and blend until smooth. Serves 2.

Cantaloupe Banana

1	Ripe banana, cut into pieces and frozen
1/4	Ripe cantaloupe, seeded
1/2 cup	Nonfat or low fat yogurt
2 tablespoon	Skim milk powder
1 1/2 tablespoon	Orange juice concentrate
2 teaspoon	Honey

Combine all of the ingredients in a blender and blend until smooth.

Cantaloupe Raspberry

1/2	Cantaloupe, seeded, cut into pieces
1 cup	Raspberries
1/2 cup	Plain yogurt
3 tablespoons	White sugar

Combine all of the ingredients in a blender and blend until smooth. Serves 2.

Carrot Apple Banana

2 cups	Carrot juice
1/2 cup	Apple juice
1	Banana
6 ounces	Frozen nonfat vanilla or plain yogurt

Combine all of the ingredients in a blender and blend until smooth.

Chocolate Cherry Banana (Version 1)

2 tablespoons	Chocolate syrup
1 (6 oz.) container	Nonfat cherry yogurt
1	Banana, frozen
1/2 cup	Nonfat milk

Combine all of the ingredients in a blender and blend until smooth.

Chocolate Cherry Banana (Version 2)

1 (6 oz.) container	Nonfat chocolate cherry yogurt
1/4 cup	Skim milk
1	Banana
3 large	Ice cubes

Combine all of the ingredients in a blender and blend until smooth.

Coffee Banana

2 small	Bananas, cut into pieces and frozen
1-1/2 cups	Skim milk
1 (8 oz.) container	Coffee low fat yogurt
1/4 teaspoon	Ground cinnamon
dash	Ground nutmeg

Combine all of the ingredients in a blender and blend until smooth.

Note: You can garnish this smoothie with fresh banana slices and/or mint if desired.

Cranberry

1 1/2 cups	Cran-Raspberry juice
2 cups	Frozen mixed berries
1 1/2 cups	Nonfat vanilla frozen yogurt

Combine all of the ingredients in a blender and blend until smooth. Serves 2

Cranberry Strawberry Oat

1 cup	Cranberry juice
1 cup	Fresh or frozen strawberries
2/3 cup	Uncooked oats
1 (8 oz.) container	Vanilla yogurt
1 cup	Ice cubes
	Sugar to taste

Combine all of the ingredients except the ice in a blender and blend until smooth. Add the ice and blend again.

Date

1/2 cup	Dates, pitted
1/2 cup	Nonfat milk
3 tablespoons	Malt powder
1 1/2 cups	Nonfat vanilla frozen yogurt

Combine all of the ingredients in a blender and blend until smooth. Serves 2.

Fast Breakfast

1 (16 oz.) container	Low fat blueberry or strawberry yogurt
1 1/4 cups	Skim milk
3/4 cup	Fresh or frozen blueberries or strawberries
3 tablespoons	Dry milk powder
2 teaspoons	Honey

Combine all of the ingredients in a blender and blend until smooth. Serves 4.

Note: This can be prepared ahead of time and frozen in single serving portions. When ready to use, thaw overnight in the refrigerator. Stir well before drinking.

Frosty Berries

1 cup	Sugar free vanilla ice cream or frozen yogurt
1 cup	Skim milk
1/2 cup	Sugar free preserves or jam, any flavor
1 cup	Sugar free lemon-lime soda

Combine all of the ingredients in a blender and blend until smooth.

Note: You can garnish the smoothies with fresh mint leaves if desired.

Fruit Cream

1/2 cup	Nonfat vanilla yogurt
1/4 cup	Skim milk
1	Banana, frozen
1/2 cup	Raspberries, frozen
1/2 cup	Strawberries, frozen
1 tablespoon	Maple syrup

Combine all of the ingredients in a blender and blend until smooth.

Hawaiian (Version 1)

1 cup	Passion fruit nectar
1 cup	Guava nectar
1 cup	Orange sherbet
4 tablespoons	Coconut milk
1/2	Banana, frozen, cut in pieces
1/2 cup	Frozen strawberries
1/2 cup	Frozen mango slices
1 cup	Strawberry yogurt

Combine all of the ingredients in a blender and blend until smooth. Serves 3-5.

Hawaiian (Version 2)

1 cup	Pineapple, peeled, cubed
1 cup	Papaya, peeled, cubed
1/2 cup	Pineapple juice or papaya nectar
1	Ripe banana cut into pieces
1/2 cup	Nonfat vanilla yogurt
1/8-1/4 teaspoon	Coconut extract

Combine all of the ingredients in a blender and blend until smooth.

Healthy Breakfast

2 cups	Plain yogurt
1 cup	Orange juice
1 cup	Grapes
1	Apple
1-2 small	Bananas
12	Walnuts, shelled
1 large piece	Shredded wheat or 1/2 cup Grape Nuts cereal

Combine all of the ingredients in a blender and blend until smooth.

Note: For variation, you can add frozen or fresh fruit. Good options include orange, peach, dried apricots (can be soaked in the orange juice), kiwi, melon.

Lemon

2 cups	Lemonade
1 cup	Lemon yogurt
1 1/2 cups	Frozen pineapple chunks
1 cup	Pineapple sherbet

Combine all of the ingredients in a blender and blend until smooth. Serves 3-5.

Lemon Apple Honey

1/4 cup	Lemon juice
1/2 cup	Apple cider
1 medium	Apple, peeled, cored, and chopped
1	Banana
2-3 tablespoons	Honey
1 cup	Nonfat or vanilla frozen yogurt

Combine all of the ingredients in a blender and blend until smooth. Serves 2

Lemon Melon

1 1/2 cups	Honeydew melon, diced
1/2 cup	Nonfat lemon yogurt
1 cup	Frozen green grapes
1 tablespoon	Fresh mint, chopped
	Fresh lemon juice to taste (optional)

Combine all of the ingredients in a blender and blend until smooth. Serves 2

Lemon Peach

1 container	Lemon Chiffon yogurt
1	Fresh peach or 1 small can of peaches
2-4	Ice cubes

Combine all of the ingredients in a blender and blend until smooth. Serve with a dash of nutmeg on top as a garnish.

Lemon Strawberry

1 1/2 cups	Strawberries
1 tablespoon	Lemon juice
1/2 teaspoon	Lemon zest
1 cup	Nonfat vanilla yogurt
1/2 cup	Ice, crushed

Combine all of the ingredients in a blender and blend until smooth.

Lime Melon

1 cup	Vanilla lowfat yogurt
1 1/2 cups	Watermelon, chopped
1 1/2 cups	Honeydew melon, chopped
2 tablespoons	Lime juice
1 cup	Ice cubes

Combine all of the ingredients in a blender and blend until smooth. Serves 4

Mango (Version 1)

1	Ripe mango, peeled, pitted, chopped
3/4 cup	Skim milk
1/4 cup	Nonfat vanilla yogurt
3/4 teaspoon	Vanilla extract
3	Ice cubes

Combine all of the ingredients in a blender and blend until smooth. Serve with fresh mint as a garnish.

Mango (Version 2)

2	Mangos, peeled and chopped
1 cup	Mango nectar
2 cups	Nonfat vanilla yogurt
1/4 teaspoon	Cardamom

Combine all of the ingredients in a blender and blend until smooth. Serves 2

Mango Ginger

2	Ripe mangos, peeled and chopped
1 ounce	Crystallized ginger
1 cup	Nonfat buttermilk
1 (8 oz.) container	Nonfat vanilla yogurt
Handful	Ice, crushed

Combine all of the ingredients in a blender and blend until smooth. Serves 2

Mixed Berry

1/2 cup	Frozen strawberries
1/2 cup	Frozen blueberries
1/2 cup	Frozen raspberries
1/2 cup	Apple juice
1/2 teaspoon	Lemon juice
1/2 cup	Nonfat frozen yogurt
1/2 cup	Ice

Combine all of the ingredients in a blender and blend until smooth.

Nectarine

1/2 cup	Nectarines, peeled, pitted and sliced
1/4 cup	Orange juice
1/2 cup	Plain, low fat yogurt
	Honey to taste

Combine all of the ingredients in a blender and blend until smooth.

Nectarine Banana

3	Nectarines, peeled, pitted and sliced
2	Bananas, sliced
1 cup	Nonfat vanilla yogurt
2 tablespoons	Grenadine
	Ice, crushed

Combine all of the ingredients except the ice and grenadine in a blender and blend until smooth. Fill serving glasses one quarter full of crushed ice. Pour the grenadine over the ice and then add the smoothie mixture. Serves 2

Nectarine Peach

1	Nectarine
1 (6 oz.) container	Fat free peach frozen yogurt
1/2 cup	Pineapple/orange/guava juice
1/2 cup	Sugar free lemonade

Combine all of the ingredients in a blender and blend until smooth.

Orange

2	Oranges, peeled and sectioned
1	Banana, cut into pieces and frozen
1/4 cup	Orange juice
2 tablespoons	Yogurt
1 teaspoon	Vanilla extract

Combine all of the ingredients in a blender and blend until smooth. Serves 2.

Papaya

2	Ripe papayas, peeled, seeded, chopped
1/2 cup	Orange juice
1/2 cup	Vanilla frozen yogurt

Combine all of the ingredients in a blender and blend until smooth.

Papaya Nectarine

1 (6 oz.) container	Fat free peach yogurt, frozen
1	Nectarine, pitted and unpeeled
1 cup	Papaya, seeded and peeled
1 cup	Sugar free lemonade

Combine all of the ingredients in a blender and blend until smooth.

Papaya Orange Banana

1/2 medium	Papaya, peeled, seeded
3/4 cup	Orange juice
1/2	Banana
3/4 cup	Nonfat yogurt
1 teaspoon	Lime juice
3-4	Ice cubes

Combine all of the ingredients in a blender and blend until smooth.

Parfait

1/2 small	Mango, chopped
1/3 cup	Fat free lemon yogurt
1	Ice cube
1/2 small	Banana
1/3 cup	Fat free lemon yogurt
1/3 cup	Berries
1	ice cube

Combine the mango, first 1/3 cup of yogurt and ice cube in a blender and blend until smooth. Pour into serving glass.

Combine the banana, second 1/3 cup of yogurt, berries and ice cube in a blender and blend until smooth. Carefully pour into serving glass on top of the mango layer.

Note: You can garnish with extra berries on top if desired.

Peach

2 cups	Peach nectar or apple juice
1 cup	Peach yogurt
1 1/2 cups	Frozen peach slices
1/2	Banana
1 cup	Vanilla frozen yogurt

Combine all of the ingredients in a blender and blend until smooth. Serves 3-5.

Note: You can sprinkle the top with nutmeg as a garnish if desired.

Peach Blueberry

1	Peach, frozen
10	Blueberries, frozen
1 cup	Fat free frozen vanilla yogurt
1/2 cup	Low fat milk
1/2 tablespoon	Pecans, crushed
1/2 teaspoon	Salt
1/4 teaspoon	Vanilla extract

Combine all of the ingredients in a blender and blend until smooth.

Peach Breakfast

1 cup	Peaches, sliced
1 cup	Low fat vanilla yogurt
1/4 cup	Wheat germ
1/4 cup	Orange juice
1 cup	Ice cubes

Combine all of the ingredients in a blender and blend until smooth.

Peach Cinnamon

2	Ripe peaches, sliced
2 cups	Nonfat plain yogurt
3 tablespoons	Brown sugar
1/4 teaspoon	Ground cinnamon
1 cup	Ice cubes

Combine all of the ingredients in a blender and blend until smooth. Serves 2

Peach Cranberry

1 large can	Peaches, drained
1 cup	Cranberry juice
1/2 cup	Plain yogurt
1 cup	Ice, crushed

Combine all of the ingredients in a blender and blend until smooth. Serves 4.

Peach Melba

1 cup	Ripe peaches, peeled, sliced
1/4 cup	Raspberries, fresh or frozen
1 cup	Peach juice or nectar, chilled
1/2 cup	Vanilla yogurt
3	Ice cubes

Combine all of the ingredients in a blender and blend until smooth. Serves 2.

Peach Melon

1 cup	Peach nonfat yogurt
1/2 cup	Cantaloupe
1/2 cup	Honey dew melon
1/2 cup	Watermelon
1 cup	Skim milk
4	Ice cubes

Combine all of the ingredients in a blender and blend until smooth.

Peach Raspberry

1 cup	Sliced peaches, frozen
1/2 cup	Raspberries, frozen
1/2 cup	Apple juice
1/2 cup	Nonfat vanilla yogurt
1 1/2 cups	Ice, crushed

Combine all of the ingredients in a blender and blend until smooth. Serves 2.

Note: For extra peach flavor, use peach yogurt instead of vanilla.

Peanut Butter Banana

2 tablespoons	Reduced fat creamy peanut butter
1	Banana, frozen, cut into pieces
1 cup	Skim milk
1/2 cup	Frozen vanilla yogurt or fat free ice cream

Combine all of the ingredients in a blender and blend until smooth. Serves 2.

Pear

1 1/2 cups	Pears, diced
1/2 cup	Pear nectar
1/2 cup	Peach yogurt
1 teaspoon	Lemon juice
1/4 teaspoon	Fresh ginger, grated
3-5	Ice cubes

Combine all of the ingredients in a blender and blend until smooth.

Pina Colada (Version 1)

1 (6 oz.) container	Nonfat coconut yogurt, frozen
1/2	Banana, frozen
1/2 (20 oz.) can	Crushed pineapple
1 cup	Nonfat milk

Combine all of the ingredients in a blender and blend until smooth.

Pina Colada (Version 2)

2 cups	Fresh pineapple, cubed, slightly frozen
1 1/2 cups	Pineapple juice, chilled
1/4 cup	Cream of coconut
1 cup	Vanilla fat free frozen yogurt
1 cup	Ice cubes

Combine all of the ingredients in a blender and blend until smooth.

Pineapple

2 cups	Pineapple juice
2 medium	Ripe bananas, sliced
2 (8 oz.) containers	Vanilla yogurt
1 cup	Strawberries, fresh or frozen
1 tablespoon	Vanilla extract
1/4 cup	Wheat germ (optional)

Combine all of the ingredients in a blender and blend until smooth. Serves 4.

Pineapple Berry

1/4 cup	Pineapple juice
1 cup	Orange juice
2	Canned pineapple slices
6	Fresh strawberries
12-15	Frozen raspberries
8-10	Frozen boysenberries
12-15	Frozen blueberries
3 ounces	Nonfat yogurt, any flavor
	Ice

Combine all of the ingredients in a blender and blend until smooth.

Pineapple Orange Banana

1 (6 oz.) can	Pineapple orange banana juice
1	Banana
1 (6 oz.) container	Nonfat peach yogurt, frozen

Combine all of the ingredients in a blender and blend until smooth.

Pistachio Banana

1 container	Plain nonfat yogurt
4-6 tablespoons	Pistachio instant pudding mix
1	Ripe banana
1/4 cup	Skim milk
handful	Ice, crushed

Combine all of the ingredients in a blender and blend until smooth.

Power Up

1/2	Banana
1/2 cup	Nonfat vanilla yogurt
1/2 cup	Fruit juice
1 tablespoon	Soy protein powder
1 tablespoon	Molasses
1 teaspoon	Wheat germ
	Frozen fruit

Combine all of the ingredients in a blender and blend until smooth.

Note: The fruit juice can be any variety you like. Add any frozen fruit of your choice as much as needed for the consistency of smoothie you like best.

Raspberry (Version 1)

1/2 cup	Raspberries
1/4 cup	Orange juice
1/2 cup	Plain low fat yogurt
	Honey to taste

Combine all of the ingredients in a blender and blend until smooth.

Raspberry (Version 2)

1 cup	Raspberries
1 cup	Milk
1/2 cup	Yogurt
	Sugar or honey to taste

Combine all of the ingredients in a blender and blend until smooth.

Raspberry (Version 3)

1 1/2 cups	Frozen raspberries
2 1/2 cups	Orange juice
1 cup	Raspberry sherbet

Combine all of the ingredients in a blender and blend until smooth. Serves 3-5.

Raspberry Cappuccino

1 cup	Raspberries
1/3 cup	Fresh brewed espresso
3/4 cup	Low fat chocolate milk
2 tablespoons	Chocolate syrup
1 1/2 cups	Nonfat coffee flavor frozen yogurt
1/2 cup	Skim milk
1/4 teaspoon	Cocoa powder

Combine all of the ingredients except the milk and cocoa powder in a blender and blend until smooth. Pour the mixture into two glasses and set aside.

Rinse the blender. Pour the milk into the rinsed blender and blend on high speed until frothy, about 15 seconds. Divide the frothy milk between the two glasses and sprinkle the top with chocolate powder. Serves 2.

Raspberry Cream

1 1/2 cups	Frozen raspberries
1 cup	Orange juice
1 cup	Raspberry yogurt
1 cup	Vanilla frozen yogurt
1/2	Banana, cut into pieces and frozen

Combine all of the ingredients in a blender and blend until smooth. Serves 3-5.

Sparkling Fruit

1 cup	Yogurt, plain or fruit flavored
2 cup	Fresh fruit, chopped
Pinch	Nutmeg
2/3 cup	Ice cold champagne, sparkling water or ginger ale

Combine the yogurt, fruit and nutmeg in a blender and blend until smooth. Pour into two glasses, filling them 3/4 full. Top off with the champagne, sparkling water or ginger ale and gently stir to combine.

Note: Garnish each serving with mint sprigs or fruit slices, if desired. Serves 2.

This is the smoothie pictured at the start of this section.

Strawberry (Version 1)

1	Banana, cut in half and frozen
4-5	Frozen strawberries
1 (6 oz.) container	Strawberry or strawberry/banana yogurt

Combine all of the ingredients in a blender and blend until smooth. Serves 2.

Strawberry (Version 2)

5 large	Strawberries
1 (6 oz.) container	Fat free strawberry yogurt, frozen
4 ounces	Sugar free lemonade

Combine all of the ingredients in a blender and blend until smooth.

Strawberry Banana (Version 1)

1 cup	Strawberry nectar or apple juice
1 cup	Milk
1	Banana, frozen
1 1/2 cups	Frozen strawberries
1 cup	Strawberry yogurt

Combine all of the ingredients in a blender and blend until smooth. Serves 3-5.

Strawberry Banana (Version 2)

1 cup	Fresh Strawberries
1	Banana
1 cup	Nonfat yogurt
1 packet	Sugar or sugar substitute
2 cups	Ice

Combine all of the ingredients in a blender and blend until smooth.

Strawberry Banana Tofu

1 cup	Strawberries, fresh or frozen, sliced
1	Banana, cut into 1 inch pieces
4 ounces (1/2 cup)	Soft tofu, drained
1/2 cup	Apple juice
1/2 cup	Frozen vanilla nonfat yogurt
1 teaspoon	Honey
1/2 cup	Ice cubes
	Fresh whole berries for garnish

Combine all of the ingredients except the ice in a blender and blend until smooth. Add the ice and blend again.

Note: For variation, substitute peach sorbet for the frozen yogurt and peaches for the strawberries.

Strawberry Grape

1 1/2 cups	Frozen vanilla yogurt
1/8 cup	Strawberry reduced sugar jelly
1 1/2 tablespoons	Reduced Sugar Concord Grape Jelly
1/4 cup	Milk

Combine all of the ingredients in a blender and blend until smooth.

Note: If desired, you can double one or other of the jellies and eliminate the other.

Strawberry Lemon Zing

2 cups	Frozen strawberries
1 cup	Strawberry yogurt
2 cups	Lemonade

Combine all of the ingredients in a blender and blend until smooth. Serves 3-5.

Strawberry Mango

1 container	Strawberry/mango yogurt
1 cup	Fresh strawberries, cut up
1 cup	Ice cubes, crushed

Combine all of the ingredients except the ice in a blender and blend until smooth. Add the ice and blend again.

Note: You can make this with any flavor of yogurt and use the same fresh fruit instead of the strawberries.

Strawberry Peach

1 cup	Strawberries
2/3 cup	Peach yogurt
1 cup	Ice, crushed

Combine all of the ingredients in a blender and blend until smooth.

Strawberry Pineapple

3/4 bag	Frozen unsweetened whole strawberries
4 cups	Pineapple juice
1 cup	Orange juice
1 1/2 cups	Lowfat vanilla yogurt, frozen

Combine all of the ingredients in a blender and blend until smooth.

Tangerine Strawberry

1/2 cup	Tangerine juice
1/2 cup	Frozen unsweetened strawberries
1/2 cup	Lowfat or nonfat plain yogurt
1 tablespoon	Sugar, or to taste

Combine all of the ingredients in a blender and blend until smooth.

Tropical (Version 1)

1 cup	Frozen pineapple pieces
1/2	Banana
1/2 cup	Orange juice
2 tablespoons	Coconut milk
1/2 teaspoon	Lime juice
1/2 cup	Nonfat frozen vanilla yogurt
1/2 cup	Ice

Combine all of the ingredients in a blender and blend until smooth.

Tropical (Version 2)

1 1/2 cups	Tropical V-8 Splash or other pineapple/citrus juice
1/2	Banana
1/4 cup	Plain nonfat yogurt
1/4 cup	Tofu
1/2 cup	Strawberries and/or pineapple chunks
–Optional–	
3-4	Baby carrots
1 tablespoon	Wheat germ or almonds, diced

Combine all of the ingredients in a blender and blend until smooth.

Tropical (Version 3)

1 1/2 cups	Pineapple orange juice
1 cup	Sliced bananas
3/4 cup	Pineapple, diced
1/2 cup	Vanilla fat free frozen yogurt
1 tablespoon	Flaked sweetened coconut
1 cup	Ice cubes

Combine all of the ingredients in a blender and blend until smooth.

Tropical Tofu Berry

1 cup	Fat free vanilla yogurt
1 cup	Skim milk
1	Banana
3" cube	Soft tofu
3/4 cup	Blueberries
1 cup	Strawberries

Put yogurt, milk, banana, and tofu into blender and blend until smooth. Add berries and blend again.

Green Smoothies

If you're new to "going green" it's helpful to know that one of the best ways to start is with romaine lettuce or spinach. They are very mild flavors while giving you all the nutritious value that made you want to try green smoothies in the first place!

You'll notice that not all of these smoothies turn out green! For variety try the Blueberry Celery and the Berry Beet.

Avocado and banana add a creamy texture to the smoothie. If you freeze the banana first, your smoothie will be even creamier and colder. To adjust the thickness, you can add more liquid or fruit as needed.

Apple Cinnamon Romaine

1/2-1 bunch	Romaine lettuce, chopped
1-2	Apples, chopped
1	Banana, cut into pieces
1/2 teaspoon	Ground cinnamon
1 cup	Water
1 cup	Ice

Combine all of the ingredients in a blender and blend until smooth.

Note: Serve with a whole cinnamon stick as garnish/stirrer if desired.

Apple Cucumber

1 cup	Apple, cut into pieces
1 cup	Cucumber, cut into pieces
1 cup	Spinach leaves, cut into pieces
1/4 cup	Mint leaves
1 1/4 cups	Water

Combine all of the ingredients in a blender and blend until smooth.

Note: You can garnish the servings with mint leaves if desired.

Arugula Ginger

	Arugula
	Ginger, chopped
2 tablespoons	Cayenne pepper
1	Cucumber, chopped
6 cups	Water

Combine all of the ingredients in a blender and blend until smooth.

Note: For variety you can add some tomatoes and/or carrots. This is the smoothie pictured at the start of this section.

Avocado Coconut

	Avocado, diced
1	Avocado, diced
1/4 cup	Cream of coconut
1/2 cup	Nonfat vanilla yogurt
1/2 cup	Whole milk
8	Ice cubes

Combine all of the ingredients in a blender and blend until smooth.

Note: Be sure to use cream of coconut not coconut milk or water which are much thinner in consistency. Cream of coconut can be found in your grocery store in the cocktail mix or ethnic foods area.

Avocado Lemon Sorrel

1/2	Avocado
2 large handfuls	Sorrel (leaves and stems)
2 tablespoons	Fresh lemon juice
3	Strawberries
2-3	Ice cubes
	Water

Combine all of the ingredients in a blender and blend until smooth.

Note: Add as much water as you want to reach the desired consistency.

Banana Fig Spinach

1	Banana, cut into pieces and frozen
4	Figs, stems removed, halved
1 1/2 – 2 cups	Fresh spinach
1 cup	Milk
2 cubes	Ice
	Sweetener of choice to taste (optional)

Combine all of the ingredients in a blender and blend until smooth.

Notes: You can substitute 1/4 cup of frozen spinach for the fresh if desired and more convenient. You can also use any type of milk including soy to suit your taste. With the fruit in this recipe, you may not need to add the sweetener. You can add it at the end if needed.

Banana Grape Spinach

1	Banana, cut into pieces
1 cup	Grapes
1/2	Apple, cored and chopped
1 (6 oz.) container	Vanilla yogurt
1 1/2 cups	Fresh spinach leaves

Combine all of the ingredients in a blender and blend until smooth.

Banana Peanut Butter Spinach

1 cup	Nonfat milk
1/2 cup	Nonfat plain yogurt
1	Banana, cut into pieces and frozen
1 tablespoon	Natural peanut butter
2 cups	Fresh spinach
1 cup	Ice cubes (optional)

Combine all of the ingredients in a blender and blend until smooth.

Banana Pineapple Orange

1	Banana, cut into pieces
1 cup	Pineapple, cut into pieces
1 cup	Orange juice
2/3 cup	Kale, chopped
1/2 cup	Spinach, chopped
1 1/2 cups	Water

Combine all of the ingredients in a blender and blend until smooth.

Berry Beet

1 medium	Beet, baked
1 cup	Fresh or frozen berries
3-4	Purple kale leaves
1/2 medium	Cucumber, peeled and cut into pieces
1 tablespoon	Fresh lime juice
1 scoop	Plain or vanilla protein powder
1 cup	Rice milk
5-10 drops	Liquid stevia or 1 packet of dry stevia

Prior to mixing the smoothie, bake the beet at 180-350 degrees until soft. Cool, peel cut it into pieces.

Combine all of the ingredients in a blender and blend until smooth.

Note: For the berries, you can use any combination of blackberries, blueberries, raspberries and strawberries.

Blueberry Celery

1-2	Bananas, cut into pieces and frozen
1-2 cups	Frozen blueberries
4-6 stalks	Celery
10-16 ounces	Coconut water

Combine all of the ingredients in a blender and blend until smooth.

Carrot Apple

2 medium	Carrots, chopped
1 medium	Apple, cored, cut into pieces
1/2 cup	Baby spinach
1 tablespoon	Fresh ginger root, peeled and chopped
4-6 ounces	Water

Combine all of the ingredients in a blender and blend until smooth.

Carrot Orange

2 large	Carrots, chopped
2	Oranges, peeled
1/2-1 inch piece	Fresh ginger root, peeled and chopped
1-2 tablespoons	Water
1/2 cup	Ice, crushed (optional)

Combine all of the ingredients in a blender and blend until smooth.

Chocolate Banana Peanut Butter

1	Banana, cut into pieces and frozen
2 tablespoons	Peanut butter
2 tablespoons	Cocoa powder
2-3 handfuls	Spinach
1-1-1/2 cups	Almond or soy milk

Combine all of the ingredients in a blender and blend until smooth.

Chocolate Raspberry Romaine

2 cups	Romaine lettuce, chopped
2 cups	Fresh or frozen raspberries
1 scoop	Cocoa powder
1 cup	Coconut water
1/4 cup	Cashews
1/4 cup	Dates, pitted and chopped
1 teaspoon	Vanilla extract
Pinch	Dried red chili pepper flakes (optional)
Pinch	Sea salt
2 cups	Ice (if using fresh fruit)

Combine all of the ingredients in a blender and blend until smooth.

Coconut Banana Cream Pie

2 cups	Coconut water
1/2 cup	Unsweetened shredded coconut
4 large	Bananas
2 cups	Romaine lettuce, chopped
1/4 cup	Cashews
1-2	Dates, pitted and chopped
1 teaspoon	Vanilla extract
Pinch	Sea salt

Combine all of the ingredients in a blender and blend until smooth.

Note: You can substitute 4 drops of liquid stevia in place of the dates if desired.

Lemon Lime

1/2 medium	Lemon, peeled and deseeded
1/2 medium	Lime, peeled and deseeded
2 medium	Bananas, cut into pieces
1/4 cup	Fresh squeezed orange juice
1-2 cups	Kale or spinach, chopped (optional)

Combine all of the ingredients in a blender and blend until smooth.

Melon Grape Broccoli

3 cups	Honeydew melon, peeled, seeded and cut into pieces
1 cup	Green grapes
1	Cucumber, peeled and chopped
1/2 cup	Broccoli florets
1 sprig	Fresh mint
3 cups	Ice cubes

Combine all of the ingredients in a blender and blend until smooth.

Raisin Kale

2 tablespoons	Raisins
2 tablespoons	Ground flax
1	Banana
1 handful	Kale
1 tablespoon	Peanut butter
1 tablespoon	Agave nectar or honey
1 cup	Almond milk
5	Ice cubes

Combine all of the ingredients in a blender and blend until smooth.

Spicy Avocado

3 cups	Water
1	Avocado
1 small	Orange beet
1 small	Cucumber
4-6 stalks	Collard greens
2 tablespoons	Fresh lemon juice
1/8 teaspoon	Vanilla extract
1" piece	Fresh ginger, peeled and chopped
1/2	Jalapeno pepper

Combine all of the ingredients in a blender and blend until smooth.

Note: Use more or less of the jalapeno pepper to suit your taste for the spicy!

Strawberry Banana Kiwi

1 cup	Strawberries
1	Banana, cut into pieces
3-4	Kiwi, peeled and cut into pieces
1 cup	Spinach, chopped
2 cups	Water

Combine all of the ingredients in a blender and blend until smooth.

White Peach Orange Romaine

2	Oranges, peeled and cut into pieces
1	White peach, pitted and chopped
4-6 large	Romaine leaves
1 cup	Ice

Combine all of the ingredients in a blender and blend until smooth.

Smoothies with a Kick

These are for adults only and definitely NOT for breakfast!
They all contain a kick of alcohol but of course you can make a
virgin version as well. Just add an equal amount of liquid in
place of the alcohol.

Banana Rum

2 large	Bananas
1/4 cup	Low fat milk
1 1/2 cups	Nonfat vanilla frozen yogurt
2 tablespoons	Light rum
2 tablespoons	White crème de cacao
2 tablespoons	Banana liqueur

Combine all of the ingredients in a blender and blend until
smooth. Serves 2

Bloody Mary

2 small	Tomatoes
1	Cucumber, peeled and chopped
1 stalk	Celery, chopped
1 large	Carrot, chopped
2 teaspoon	Onion, chopped
1/4 cup	Fresh cilantro leaves
1 cup	Ice cubes
2 ounces	Vodka
1 teaspoon	Black pepper (optional)
	Hot sauce and/or to taste (optional)

Combine all of the ingredients in a blender and blend until smooth.

Brandy Alexander

1	Banana
1 cup	Vanilla Ice Cream
4 ounces	Brandy
4 ounces	Crème de Cacao
	Ground Nutmeg

Combine all of the ingredients except the nutmeg in a blender and blend until smooth. Sprinkle the nutmeg on top before serving.

Eggnog

1	Banana, cut into pieces
1 cup	Nonfat plain yogurt
1 cup	Light eggnog
1 cup	Ice cubes
1 ounce	Bourbon
1 ounce	Brandy
	Ground nutmeg

Combine all of the ingredients except the nutmeg in a blender and blend until smooth. Sprinkle the nutmeg on top before serving.

Note: This is the smoothie pictured at the start of this section.

Irish Coffee

1 cup	Whole milk
2-8 ounces	Coffee yogurt
1 1/3 cup	Cold coffee
1/4-1/2 cup	Bailey's Irish Cream, to taste
2 tablespoons	Irish whiskey

Combine all of the ingredients in a blender and blend until smooth.

Margarita

3/4 cup	Orange sorbet or sherbet
1 cup	Mango, diced
2 tablespoons	Tequila
1 teaspoon	Triple sec
1 tablespoon	Grand marnier

Combine all of the ingredients in a blender and blend until smooth.

Mimosa

4 ounces	Orange juice concentrate, frozen
1/2 cup	Low fat milk
1/2 ounce	Vanilla yogurt
2 ounces	Orange yogurt
1/2 cup	Vanilla vodka
1/8 cup	Orange flavored liqueur
1 cup	Ice cubes, crushed

Combine all of the ingredients in a blender and blend until smooth. Serves 2.

Mojito

5 ounces	Seven Up soda
2.5 ounces	White Rum
2 ounces	Lime juice
2 tablespoons	Raw sugar
4-5	Ice cubes, crushed
2 branches	Fresh mint leaves

Combine all of the ingredients in a blender and blend until smooth. Serves 2.

Note: Garnish the smoothie with the mint leaves if desired.

Pina Colada

1	Banana, cut into pieces and frozen
1/2 (20 oz.) can	Crushed pineapple
16 ounces	Unsweetened coconut milk
2 teaspoons	Honey
4 ounces	Rum

Combine all of the ingredients in a blender and blend until smooth.

Note: Use a pineapple wedge and a cherry for garnish if desired.

Raspberry Amaretto

3 ounces	Raspberries, fresh or frozen thawed
1 cup	Vanilla ice cream
1/2 tablespoons	Amaretto
1/2 teaspoons	Orange zest
	Ice
2	Amarettini cookies, crumbled

Combine all of the ingredients in a blender and blend until smooth. Use as much ice as needed to reach the desired consistency.

Sprinkle the cookies over the top for a garnish.

Note: This is the one pictured at the start of this section.

Tequila Sunrise

1 cup	Orange sorbet or sherbet
2 tablespoons	Fresh orange juice
6 tablespoons	Tequila
2 teaspoons	Grenadine
4	Ice cubes

Combine all of the ingredients in a blender and blend until smooth. Garnish with an orange slice if desired.

Tropical Island

3/4 cup	Pineapple juice
1	Banana
1	Peach
2 tablespoons	Whipped cream
4 ounces	Coconut Rum
1 tablespoon	Honey
1 cup	Ice

Combine all of the ingredients in a blender and blend until smooth.

Strawberry Daiquiri

1 cup	Strawberry sorbet or sherbet
1/2 tsp	Lime juice
1 teaspoon	Orange juice
4	Fresh strawberries
5 tablespoons	White rum
4	Ice cubes, crushed

Combine all of the ingredients in a blender and blend until smooth. Garnish with one whole or sliced strawberry if desired.

New Year

1 cup	Plain yogurt
1 cup	Strawberries
6 ounces	Champagne
4	Ice Cubes, crushed

Combine all of the ingredients in a blender and blend until smooth.

Wine Mango Cooler

6 ounces	Mango, chopped
10 ounces	White Wine
2-4 tablespoons	Raw Sugar, to taste
4	Ice Cubes, crushed

Combine all of the ingredients in a blender and blend until smooth.

White Russian

1/2 cup	Vanilla ice cream
3 tablespoons	Vodka
3 tablespoons	Crème de cacao
4	Ice cubes, crushed
1 dash	Ground nutmeg

Combine all of the ingredients except the nutmeg in a blender and blend until smooth. Sprinkle the nutmeg on top before serving.

About the Author

Cathy L. Kidd is a craftsperson at heart. For as long as she can remember she has been creating things with her hands. She has done crochet (taught to her by her Aunt Carol), stained glass (learned by taking a class), candlemaking (learned from an ebook) and cooking (learned initially from Betty Crocker!)

Her homemade recipe books specialize in recipes for your kitchen appliances, in this case your blender. Her other books include:

- Homemade Bread Recipes – A Simple and Easy Bread Machine Cookbook
- How to Make Homemade Bread – Simple and Easy Bread Making Tips and Recipes
- Homemade Soup Recipes: Simple and Easy Slow Cooker Recipes
- How to Make Homemade Ice Cream: Simple and Easy Ice Cream Maker Recipes

This time, her smoothie book gives you simple and easy recipes in a lot of smoothie categories. There should be something for everyone in your family to enjoy.
For more recipes visit: www.easyhomemadebreadrecipes.com.

19049043R00056

Made in the USA
Middletown, DE
31 March 2015